bAjc
5
08

LINE OF DUTY

THE U.S. BORDER PATROL

GUARDING THE NATION

by Connie Colwell Miller

Reading Consultant
Barbara J. Fox
Reading Specialist
North Carolina State University

Content Consultant
Kenneth E. deGraffenreid
Professor of Intelligence Studies
Institute of World Politics
Washington, D.C.

Capstone
press

Mankato, Minnesota

Blazers is published by Capstone Press,
151 Good Counsel Drive, P.O. Box 669, Mankato, Minnesota 56002.
www.capstonepress.com

Library of Congress Cataloging-in-Publication Data
Miller, Connie Colwell, 1976–
    The U.S. Border Patrol: guarding the nation / by Connie Colwell Miller.
    p. cm. — (Blazers. Line of duty)
    Summary: "Describes the activities and duties of the Border Patrol in
defending the borders of the United States" — Provided by publisher.
    Includes bibliographical references and index.
    ISBN–13: 978-1-4296-1270-8 (hardcover)
    ISBN–10: 1-4296-1270-3 (hardcover)
    1. Border patrols — United States — Juvenile literature. 2. U.S. Customs
and Border Protection — Juvenile literature. I. Title. II. Series.
JV6483.M543 2008
363.28'50973 — dc22   2007025099

Editorial Credits
Aaron Sautter, editor; Bobbi J. Wyss, designer; Wanda Winch, photo researcher

Photo Credits
AP Images/David Maung, 13 (top); Dennis Poroy, 24 (top); Duluth News Tribune/
    Derek Neas, 24 (bottom); El Paso Times/Victor Calzada, 10–11; Immigration
    and Naturalization Service, 13 (bottom); John Miller, 25; Lennox McLendon,
    28–29; Matt York, 15
Corbis/Ann Johansson, 8–9, 18; Greg Smith, 17; Reuters/Carlos Barria, 4–5;
    Fred Greaves, 6; Shaul Schwarz, cover;.
Getty Images Inc./AFP/Omar Torres, 16; David McNew, 12; Joe Raedle, 14; Manuel
    Ocano, 26–27; Time & Life Pictures/Mai/Dave Gatley, 22–23
The Image Works/Bob Strong, 19
Landov LLC/Reuters/Rick Wilking, 20–21

1 2 3 4 5 6 13 12 11 10 09 08

TABLE OF CONTENTS

WATCHING THE NIGHT

It's a dark night in Texas. Some people are trying to sneak across the Mexican **border**. They want to enter the United States.

[**border** — the dividing line between one country and another]

5

A U.S. Border Patrol agent sees movement in the dark. He calls for help on his radio.

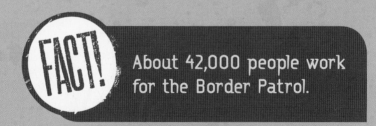

FACT! About 42,000 people work for the Border Patrol.

More agents zoom to the scene. They arrest the people crossing the border. Then the agents send the people back to their own country.

PROTECTING OUR BORDERS

The Border Patrol is part of the Department of Homeland Security. The Border Patrol stops people from entering the United States without **permission**.

[**permission** — the okay to do something]

People try to sneak into the
United States in many ways. Some
swim across deep rivers. Others crawl
through tunnels. A few even hide in
strange places inside vehicles.

The United States shares
borders with Canada and Mexico.
These borders cover almost 7,000
miles (11,265 kilometers). Agents
protect the land along the borders.

Canadian border

Mexican border

FACT! The Border Patrol also protects the coastlines of Florida and Puerto Rico.

Agents stop traffic at **checkpoints**. They ask people for identification. They search vehicles for drugs and weapons.

[**checkpoint** — a spot on the border where vehicles are stopped for inspection]

Traffic checkpoint at Tijuana, Mexico

Dogs help search for drugs and weapons.

EQUIPMENT AND VEHICLES

Agents watch the borders with video cameras and computers. Computers sound alarms when someone crosses the border.

Most people try to cross the U.S. border at night. Agents use night-vision cameras to see people moving in the dark.

U.S. Customs and Border Protection

Silver Arrow

101

FACT! The Border Patrol uses remote control airplanes to watch the border.

The Border Patrol uses many vehicles. Agents drive cars, use boats, and fly planes. Some agents ride on **ATUs** or horses.

[**ATU** — all-terrain vehicle]

CATCHING CRIMINALS

Thousands of people try to enter the United States every day. Some may be criminals or **terrorists**. The Border Patrol helps keep dangerous people from entering the country.

[**terrorist** — someone who uses violence and threats to frighten people]

Benjamin
Arellano-Felix

Ramon
Arellano-Felix

Jesus
Labra-Aviles

ARELLANO-FELIX HOT LINE

Call Toll Free From USA

1-800-720-7775

Collect/Direct From Mexico

001-858-277-4215

All Calls Answered By U.S. Agents
All Calls Confidential
E-mail: afotips@k-online.com

Arturo
Paez-Martinez

Ismael
Higuera-Guerrero

WANTED

Information on the Drug Trafficking and Money Laundering Activities of the Tijuana Cartel

Eduardo
Arellano-Felix

Javier
Arellano-Felix

Gilberto
Higuera-Guerrero

Manuel
Aguirre-Galindo

Gustavo
Rivera-Martinez

The Border Patrol works hard to protect the United States. It's not easy to enter the country illegally with the Border Patrol on the job.

FACT! The Border Patrol stops almost 3,000 people from entering the country illegally every day.

GLOSSARY

ATV (AY TEE VEE) — all-terrain vehicle; ATVs have four large wheels that travel easily over rough ground.

border (BOR-duhr) — the dividing line between one country and another

checkpoint (CHEK-point) — a spot on a road or border where vehicles are stopped for inspection

identification (eye-den-tuh-fuh-KAY-shuhn) — something that proves who you are

illegal (i-LEE-guhl) — against the law

permission (pur-MISH-uhn) — the okay to do something

terrorist (TER-ur-ist) — someone who uses violence and threats to frighten people

READ MORE

Donovan, Sandra. *Protecting America: A Look at the People Who Keep Our Country Safe.* How Government Works. Minneapolis: Lerner, 2004.

Stewart, Gail B. *Illegal Immigration.* Ripped from the Headlines. San Diego: Erickson Press, 2007.

INTERNET SITES

FactHound offers a safe, fun way to find Internet sites related to this book. All of the sites on FactHound have been researched by our staff.

Here's how:
1. Visit *www.facthound.com*
2. Choose your grade level.
3. Type in this special code **1429612703** for age-appropriate sites. You may also browse subjects by clicking on letters, or by clicking on pictures and words.
4. Click on the **Fetch It** button.

FactHound will fetch the best sites for you!

INDEX